Becoming The
Iron Lady

Margaret Thatcher

Becoming The Iron Lady

Margaret Thatcher

Written by
Andrea Bohn
Illustrated by Jason Velazquez

Liberty Hill Publishing
555 Winderley Pl, Suite 225
Maitland, FL 32751
407.339.4217
www.libertyhillpublishing.com

Illustrations by: Jason Velazquez

Paperback ISBN-13: 978-1-66288-633-1
Hard Cover ISBN-13: 978-1-66288-634-8
Ebook ISBN-13: 978-1-66288-635-5

To: Ellie, Izzy, and Lydia

On October 13, 1925, Margaret Roberts was born in
Grantham, England, to Alfred and Beatrice Roberts.
She was the youngest of two children.

Margaret's father owned two grocery stores in town, and her family was very religious.

Through work and church, her parents taught her the value of hard work, discipline, and courage.

Margaret loved to read, and in school, she studied constantly to be at the top of her class. When she was ten years old, she received a scholarship to go to the best grammar school in Grantham.

When Margaret was twelve,
her sister had a pen pal named Edith.

Edith was from Austria, and was one of millions of
Jews who were in danger from the Nazis. Margaret
and her sister raised money to help Edith escape
from Austria and come to England.

Soon after Edith escaped to England, war broke out in Europe. During the war, Margaret volunteered with the Women's Volunteer Service in Grantham.

When Margaret was seventeen, she graduated from grammar school and began studying her favorite subject, science, at Oxford University.

At first, Margaret was lonely and felt like she didn't fit in with the other students. She missed her family and her home, but she continued to study hard, and eventually, she felt better.

After college, Margaret worked as a laboratory researcher, although she dreamed of working in Parliament.

While working as a researcher, Margaret decided to pursue her dreams, and became involved in local politics. Soon, she was nominated to head the political party in her area.

While leading her local political party,
Margaret met her future husband, Dennis Thatcher.
Two years later, they were married.

After Margaret and Dennis were married, Margaret decided to study law, and became pregnant. Margaret gave birth to twins and soon after, she passed her tests to become a lawyer.

After becoming a lawyer, Margaret was elected as a district representative. She had finally become an elected member of Parliament.

While she was in Parliament, Margaret achieved many great things. Margaret didn't always get along with the other members of Parliament, but her coworkers respected her.

Margaret always stood firmly for what she thought was right, and worked hard to protect the rights and liberties of the people, not only in England, but across the world. This is how she earned the nickname, "The Iron Lady."

In 1979, Margaret Thatcher became the first female Prime Minister of England.

<u>Margaret Thatcher's Greatest Achievements:</u>

May 4, 1979

Margaret Thatcher was the first female to be elected as the head of a government in Europe, and was considered, for a time, to be one of the most powerful women in the world. She is still considered to be one of the most influential people of the twentieth century.

April 30, 1980

She successfully navigated the Iranian Embassy Siege. On April 30, 1980, five armed men stormed the Iranian Embassy and held twenty-six people hostage. They demanded the release of ninety of their countrymen, and safe passage out of the U.K. Margaret Thatcher rejected their ransom, refusing to negotiate with terrorists. Instead, she approved Operation Nimrod, which was carried out by British Special Air Service (SAS) in less than seventeen minutes, and resulted in the rescue of all but one of the hostages.

October 3, 1980

Margaret Thatcher passed the Housing Act of 1980, also known as the "Right to Buy" policy in October of 1980. This act allowed citizens to purchase their housing units from their local authorities, and gave discounts to tenants who had lived at their current home for three or more years. The act affected over three million people, of which one million ended up purchasing their own housing units.

1980–1989

She reduced taxes and regulations, allowing for class mobility among the people of the U.K. During her years as Prime Minister, she reduced taxes by 25% – 40%, allowing the idea of upward mobility to become an actual possibility for the lower classes of the U.K.

June 14, 1982

She led the U.K. to victory against Argentina in the Falkland's War. In 1982, Argentina invaded the Falkland Islands, a British territory. Margaret Thatcher led the War Cabinet in Parliament that oversaw the conduct of the war, and authorized the navy to retakethe islands. Seventy-four days after the war began, Argentina surrendered, and Margaret Thatcher earned the reputation of being a highly capable war leader.

July 26, 1984

Margaret Thatcher passed reforms, particularly the Trade Union Act 1984, which helped to end militant trade unionism. Union-led strikes in the U.K. were crippling the U.K.'s economy, and Margaret Thatcher helped to pass reforms in Parliament that made union strikes, as a first action, illegal, thereby forcing unions to use other methods of negotiation before going on strike.

December 26, 1991

Margaret Thatcher is credited with playing a key role in ending the Cold War. Margaret Thatcher was the first person to suggest working with Mikhail Gorbachev to bring down the Iron Curtain. She worked to bring Ronald Reagan and Gorbachev together, resulting in the Intermediate-Range Nuclear Forces Treaty (INF). Margaret Thatcher, Ronald Reagan, and Pope John Paul II worked together closely to bring about the end of the Cold War in 1989.

Bibliography:

Aitken, Jonathan. Margaret Thatcher: Power and Personality. New York: Bloomsbury USA, 2013.

Blundell, John. Margaret Thatcher: A Portrait of the Iron Lady. New York: Algora Publishing, 2008.

Moore, Charles. Margaret Thatcher: At Her Zenith: In London, Washington and Moscow (Authorized Biography of Margaret Thatcher). New York: Alfred A. Knopf, 2019.

Printed in the USA
CPSIA information can be obtained
at www.ICGtesting.com
LVHW070326281023
762379LV00017B/148